A Quarter Century
of Poetry

Larisa Thorne

BookLeaf
Publishing

India | USA | UK

Presentation by *BookLeaf Publishing*

Web: www.bookleafpub.com

E-mail: info@bookleafpub.com

ISBN : 9789357449182

First edition 2021

DEDICATION

To my badly-neglected inner poet. May this serve as a stepping stone to more.

An Old Man with a Beard

There was once an old man with a beard,
who said, "It is just as I feared!
Two owls and a hen,
four larks and a wren,
have all made their nests in my beard!"

A Young Lady from Niger

There was once a young lady from Niger,
who smiled as she rode on a tiger.
They returned from a ride
with the lady inside
and a smile on the face of the tiger.

Rain

The sky a unilateral, unassuming slate of grey.
Colors brightened artificially by their wetness.
The steady weep, weep, weep,
down the towering oak's fingertips,
each drop suspended another moment
in spherical, glassy splendor.

The auditory stench of industry;
a keening train horn,
a grumbling car motor,
drowned into submission by the dull roar
of droplets beating the pavement.

A coffee-scented sigh escapes
the enamored observer's lips,
momentarily obscuring the translucent plane
dividing nature from her admirer.

Little table on the corner

In the hush of the January winter,
plague laying heavy as a coat,
The glint of sun on metal shone as a beacon,
beckoning the weary shut-in, just for a moment
to the little table on the corner.

Seated, feet tucked, gloves off, scone propped.
Unmasked.

Breathe in.
Breathe out.

Welcoming the new air, like a sharp blade of
winter
tempered by spring-like warmth and
distant bird caws.

Noonday sun, unfettered by clouds,
shines with fierce welcome on carelessly bare
skin.

Light alighting,

tangling,
with long, blonde locks.

Coffee roaring,
melting into rumble,
into soft, contented purr
as the minutes flaneur by,
at the little table on the corner.

The Wait

Shoulders held high,
stiff and unyielding like two mountain peaks,
yet acutely sensitive to time
flowing by in a manner most annoyingly
languorous.

Each moment bearing the seeds of anticipation,
of doubt,
of excitement,
of worry.
Which will blossom? Which will go to dust?
A secret, carefully guarded by the future.

Senses on high alert,
hands, feet, and gaze shifting.
Like an impatient crow
hopping agitatedly.
But hark
are those footsteps?

OS132

With a sudden lurch,
on a chill autumnal afternoon,
our silver, wingéd chariot bounded into the sky.
Nigh a flap, soaring into the cloud be-wisped
blue.

Through small, round portals we bespy
as soft, effervescent white puffs meander by.
A view best enjoyed
with a warm, hearty meal.
Plates neatly fitting the lapspace square
like a jigsaw puzzle, arranged with care.
A porcelain cup, single delicate golden arm
extended,
ready,
complimenting sweet slivers of cake
with its dark, earthy brew.

As the sun colors a narrow band of horizon
like a shy blush,
we descend once more down into cloud and
mystery,
leaving behind the landscape,
airy, light, and lonely,

which we would otherwise only glimpse from
far below.

Golden slumber

Dark depths glitter gold
Wingéd menace slumbers
'til halfling thief comes

Seaside drive

Tracing the gently undulating coast
in a Honda CRV,

A thousand gull cries
more menacing than a plea,

Taco and kombucha ride shotgun
as if by decree,

on this lazy summer day
by the sea.

Codex Dresdensis

Figures marching across accordion pages
in painstaking detail
With limbs of sienna and umber aglow.
Their richly beplumed heads
heavy with responsibility,
tip back,
beholding the heavens above.
As tall stalks of corn sprout
from the maw of the feathered serpent,
their named gods watch on.

On the autumnal cusp

Tall and silent
the green sentinels stand.
Light leafy fingers
heavy with dappled sunlight.
Moons upon moons spent
gathering their verdant capes full.
Quietly then, like a thief
stealing among them:
A drop of yellow. A splash of red
appears.
The nearly imperceptibly slow march
of time and color,
with a sudden brilliant and spectacular
crescendo
over.

Together

Work left safely tucked
into sleeping laptops
The setting sun warms our backs
as we thread through the Shadyside streets
Stopped only by the gentle, bready exhale
of the great Taglio oven.
At its side, we gather for the feast.
Catching sparkling jewels
of crisp white diamond,
of sweet pale gold,
of bold garnet red
in our little glasses.
Conversation overflowing its banks,
branching and rejoining fluidly
as we dip in and out of it.
Bubbles of carbonation and laughter.
The mood more merry with each sip.
When we are together, we share all we have.
And what a joy it is.

Lussekatter

14

Two yellow spirals
warm and yeasty, raisin-crowned
a taste of Christmas.

State of the universe

The state of the universe
is a curious thing.
Mysteriously capturing
everything.

From the smell of rain on a warm summer day,
to the chaotic motions of two black holes at play.

Every data
Every point
Carefully measured, recorded,
with purpose anoint.

But who is the bookkeeper?
How is it stored?
There is no satisfaction in abstraction.
There must be more!

From an orderly central library,
a programmer's dream,
to accessing everything everywhere,
egalitarian, it would seem.

Possibilities abound.
A philosophical and practical conundrum,

for us to wrap our heads around.

Darcy's Letter

Three charges were laid.
But with honesty addressed,
prideful veneer falls.

No time to rise

Cantankerously I awaken
Limbs festooned tightly by bedsheets
Eyelids unwilling to part
Morning is growing old
From these warm covers
I won't depart
without force
Good night
Zzz

To the bakery

A visit to the bakery
in morning's humble light.
Leave behind the wet, blue streets
to be greeted by its warm
yellow and orange hues.

A greeting at the door,
wrapping the traveler in fragrant embrace.
Walls lined with soft, rounded shapes.
Muted sounds of loaves sliding into
brown paper bags.
Their oven-kissed surfaces
beckoning.

A poem not about penguins

Mind drained from the day's work,
the theme for this poem was outsourced,
reluctantly.
A friend, this creative compadre,
was to give me reprieve.

"A penguin", said he.
"A penguin?", I grumbled and scoffed.

With their ungainly, lurching,
stumbling motion across the ice.
Their throaty cawing,
with all the melodiousness of flu-like croaks.
Feeding their young only the finest,
regurgitated after many miles and hours.

Hardly a dignified choice
to grace a poem.

And yet...

The next
twenty-five

A worthy challenge
Twenty-five years' poetry.
Here is to the next!

www.ingramcontent.com/pod-product-compliance
Lightning Source LLC
LaVergne TN
LVHW041302200726
843507LV00014B/3091